DANCE LIKE THE WIND

Timeless Teachings for Spiritual People

let you dreams fly!

2 Bill

BILL EAGER

Published by Redwood Publishing, LLC
Orange County, CA
www.redwooddigitalpublishing.com

Disclaimer of Warranty: The publisher and author make no representations or warranties with respect to the accuracy or completeness of the content of this book and specifically disclaim any implied warranty of fitness for a particular purpose. The advice and strategies contained herein may not be suitable for your situation. You should consult with a professional where appropriate. Neither the publisher nor author shall be liable for any loss of profit or any other damages, including but not limited to special, incidental, consequential or other damages.

The author of this book does not dispense medical advice nor prescribe the use of any technique as a form of treatment for physical or medical problems without the advice of a physician. The intent of the author is only to offer information of a general nature to help you in your quest for physical fitness and good health. In the event you use any of the information in this book for yourself, or others, which is your constitutional right, the author and the publisher assume no responsibility for your actions. Indeed, not all exercise, diet, or alternative solutions are suitable for every person. To reduce the risk of injury, consult your physician before beginning any new program. Exercises, discussions, and instructions in this book are in no way intended as a substitute for medical counseling.

Thrive Inside®
Visit: www.ThriveInside.net
Thrive Inside® is a registered trademark.

ISBN: 978-1-952106-73-6 (paperback)
ISBN: 978-1-952106-74-3 (ebook)
Library of Congress Catalog Number: 2020924839

First printing: February 2021
Printed in the United States of America

For Laurie

Acknowledgments

All of my teachers, friends, and family.

Profound teachings are shared from one generation of teachers to the next. I am happy to share what has been shared with me in what I hope is a new voice that contains the power and intention of the teachings. A special thank you to my dear friend, teacher and guru Yogi Amrit Desai whose love and wisdom is boundless. I also want to thank my readers Tom Bosma, Leslie Epstein, Cordelia Wilkerson, Rich Flowerday, Dirk Olson, and Sara Stratton.

Other Books By Bill Eager

Available on Amazon

Thrive Inside: Transformative Secrets of
Spiritual Masters, Gurus & Shamans

Contents

Introduction

This book of basic yogic principles and quotes is designed to be a touchstone for your evolution. Body, mind, heart, and spirit are never separate entities; each informs the others about their state. If you pay attention and listen carefully to the messages they send, you can create personal harmony. It is an internal harmony that is reflected in the world you live in. Learn to be at peace with yourself as you are…and the world as it is. Move through this book spontaneously, even randomly. Assimilate wisdom and relate it to your personal experience in a manner that helps you grow and share.

Words carry energy. Sometimes a simple sentence can resonate a deep understanding for a process you have been going through. It is like the missing piece in a puzzle you have been working on. It sheds new light, a new dimension, to your personal journey. You have heard it before, but this time the arrangement of the words creates a new understanding or reinforces a knowing that you have had from previous teachings and experiences.

If you teach or practice yoga, I hope some of the sayings can be used to fine-tune your practice. One concept, sentence, or word can become a foundation. *Namaste.*

Bill Eager

BODY

Much of the experience of being human comes from the fact that we are born into a physical body. There is debate about when our spirit decides to enter our body in our mother's womb, and exactly how much of the life that we are about to live has been pre-agreed in the spiritual plane. We do know that our physical being embodies us and performs a great service as it carries our spirit from our first breath in all the way to our last breath out.

Along the journey from birth to death, your physical body becomes intertwined in your story. Mental, psychological, genetic, and karmic patterns begin to have an impact on your relationship with your body. Self-image is intimately connected with your perception about the world you live in. When you love what you see in the mirror, your self-confidence is strengthened, you feel good, and you can have harmonious interpersonal relationships.

All matter is in a state of vibration. Your physical body is a vibrational state of matter. Energy is constantly moving through your *chakras* and *nadis*, the energy centers and channels. When you connect with your energy and awaken your true nature, you can move into healing naturally, organically. You can use your body as a vehicle to induce harmony in the body-mind-spirit connection.

Tap Into Your Energy With Your Breath

Breathing is job one. Stop breathing and you will be dead in ten minutes. Brain damage occurs in three. Breath is unique because it is connected to both your autonomous and voluntary nervous systems. This means breathing works automatically. For example, you continue to breathe during the night without thinking about it. You can also control your breath. In yoga, the conscious use of breath is the profound science of pranayama. *Prana* is a Sanskrit word that means energy, and *ayama* means control. Pranayama is the control of energy with breathing.

There are four stages to breathing. It is not simply in and out.

    A. You inhale (Puraka)
    B. The breath pauses for a moment (Abhyantara kumbhaka)
    C. You exhale (Rechaka), and
    D. The breath stays out for a moment (Bahya kumbhaka).

The pauses are important. When you take air in and hold it, the retention period is the time when oxygen gets absorbed into your bloodstream. The life supporting oxygen is then carried around the entire body, reaching every cell. The pause in your breath becomes a moment when you get close to being absolutely still.

The pause can increase your ability to concentrate; it can also strengthen your understanding and control over your life. All the rhythmic cycles of the universe are composed of these same movements. The universe itself expands, pauses, contracts and expands again. It just takes a little longer.

You can control:

- How deeply you breathe.
- The speed of inhalation and exhalation.
- How long you hold your breath in or out.
- Whether you breathe in or out with your nose or mouth.
- Which nostril you breathe in or out of.
- Whether you breathe in or out of your mouth with the mouth wide open or closed—like breathing from a straw.

The conscious use of breathing can influence many systems in your body. You can calm your heartbeat, reduce blood pressure and increase brain activity.

EXERCISE

Practice Good Breathing

Sit in a comfortable position or lie down on the floor or in a bed. Place your hands just below your rib cage. Proper breathing starts in the nose and then moves air down as your lungs expand. Watch as you breathe in and the air completely fills your lungs from the bottom to the top as if you are filling up a water bottle. You can feel your abdomen expand as the air moves up into the chest. Your abdomen goes down, and your chest lifts up. As you breathe out, empty the lungs from the top to the bottom, completely exhaling the old air. Notice the chest goes down first, then your abdomen follows as you complete your exhalation. Normal breathing is slow and steady, like your heartbeat. Breathe consciously for two or three minutes and begin to establish a pattern of healthy breathing.

Alternate Nostril Breathing

Alternate nostril breathing is one way to bring balance to your breath and harmony to your chakras, mind, body, and spirit. It energizes the two hemispheres of your brain, connecting your intuitive and creative right cerebrum with your logical and reasoning left cerebrum. This balance extends to your chakras. It calms your mind. It allows energy to move freely through your body, which empowers your body to access its natural healing abilities.

You may notice that when you are in a state of balance and harmony, it is reflected in your breathing. You are in balance when your breath is calm, steady, and flows easily. You are out of balance when your breathing is uneven, rapid, or congested. The many moods you have during a day are reflected and connected to variations in your breathing patterns.

The Breath Chart shows a few variations of breathing (keep in mind the numbers represent seconds). You can do these variations with both of your nostrils open, breathing through the nose. You can also do them as alternate nostril breathing. Here is how you would do it alternating:

1. Hold one nostril closed while you inhale through the other nostril.
2. Hold the air in.
3. Now, close the other nostril and exhale.
4. Hold the breath out.
5. Repeat by inhaling now with the nostril that is open, and which you did not inhale with the first time.

This opens the *ida* and *pingala* energy channels which run alongside your spine. The numbers are "counts." Advanced practitioners use yogic breathing techniques such as Kapalbhati or Bhastrika to rapidly change oxygen levels, energy and consciousness. If you have a medical condition, consult your physician before doing anything new.

Inhale	Hold	Exhale	Hold	Results
2	8	4	8	Relax
6	3	6	3	Balance
6	6	6	1	Energize

BODY

Use your body to anchor your mind into the power of the present moment.

All the wisdom of your incarnations is built into your body.

On your journey to source, you must travel through the body, not the mind, to experience the divine being you truly are. Breath is your travel companion.

A timeless spirit that comes through your time-bound body is an inborn enigma.

You spend most of your energy on managing your external world and circumstances at the sacrifice of your internal world.

When you find balance in your body you live your life like a dance, when you find balance in your mind you accept what others think, and when you find balance in your spirit you accept what others believe.

Spiritual practice is a one-way practice —you give, give, and give more.

Everything you are seeking is already inside you.

CAREER

You don't get tired by the work you do; you get tired by the resistance you bring to it.

Find the talents you have acquired in your past lives to understand your mission in this one.

Many aspects of spiritual learning do not have economic ramifications, nor should they.

DEATH

During sleep part of your astral body leaves and moves to the same space as those that have passed.

When you start to surround yourself with comfort, making life always comfortable, you are preparing for death.

The soul must shed desires in the astral world as fulfillment is impossible there.

EXPERIENCE

The way you experience life is your creation.

Knowledge and experience are two wings of a bird. You need both. With one, you fall.

Do not dismiss the authentic experience of another person; and do not dismiss your own experience.

Look at all the costumes that *Shakti*, the energy of the universe, adorns herself with for your pleasure: movement, thought, feelings, silence, intuition. Watch as the larger life around you becomes the dance.

GURU

A guru embodies what they teach from their own experience.

GU is the darkest of nights and RU is the radiant light.

LEADERSHIP

If you are a leader you must be able to lead your own life.

LIFE ON PLANET EARTH

It is impossible to stabilize the world around you because the nature of the universe is perpetual motion.

This plane is the school for the soul to know itself. Any suffering you experience is designed for you to learn something.

MUDRAS

Because the five fingers represent the five elements they can open and close pathways in your body.

NUTRITION

You are what you eat, and food is medicine.

POLARITY

Every physical thing in the universe is a manifestation of energy as male and female; and it is available for you to access for the purpose of connecting back to the source.

The male energy in all of us is the seed of ideas and creation. Our female energy gives birth.

PRANA

Your energy follows your attention.

Tune into your body's energy and tune into universal laws.

Energy can take any form. It always looks for a vessel.

Energy travels through time and space. It never dies, only the images you attach to it change.

Energy relates directly to energy, but not through the medium of the mind.

Energy is restored in service, not in self-importance.

It takes more energy to be fragmented than focused because each fragment requires energy.

Invisible source becomes visible through prana. It is the medium through which consciousness becomes manifest.

Follow the spontaneous movement of prana.

Air and food are vehicles for prana.

Fall in love with prana. Sensations are the language the body uses to communicate with you.

Prana connects your body to your soul. To access prana, you need to be in a non-doing space.

Biological prana is subconscious and connected to breath. When your prana is unconscious it manifests as a tightness in the physical body.

Prana creates miracles because it is not related to cause and effect. It is a direct connection to God.

Prana is the energetic expression of the unmanifest, the vital life force.

You lose prana when your mind dwells on things that are outside your circle of influence.

You open yourself to prana by keeping your mind unattached to opinions, thoughts and objects.

When prana is enslaved by your fragmented mind, it is reduced. You are tired and stressed.

When you remove your mind from superimposing thoughts and emotions on your prana body, you achieve polarity. When you consciously achieve this harmony of body, mind and spirit, you can layer intention onto your prana body for integration. Pass your intention over to your higher power where your ego is not in control. Your consciousness descends into the prana.

With significant joy or grief there is a large outburst of prana which may be uncontrollable. At such times be alert to the flow of your prana. Focus on creating harmony and balance in your mind which controls the flow of prana. Remain a witness to go beyond yourself and return to your prana body.

RELATIONSHIPS

Recognize spirit in all things, seen and unseen; and know that when a person comes into your life it is magical and for your learning and dancing.

Often you want something from another person so you can be happy with yourself.

If someone hurts you, don't process it into your body. Let it go.

Friends always nurture your habits...good and bad.

If someone you love makes you *not* want to do something that you love, there is a problem.

Our connection to reality is often based on the medium of language; and the power of language is the ability to share our stories.

RESPONSIBILITY

You must be responsible for moving towards your destiny.

Prayer comes with the responsibility to act on the prayer—to give it life.

Everyone has a life force energy and how our life unfolds affects our life force energy.

You come to this world for a special purpose.

Change your perception about yourself. This allows you to create your life. See who you are and acknowledge your participation in your evolution.

THE PAST

Respect the past but do not be a hostage to old viewpoints. Your father, mother, lover, children, friends. All their views speak through you today.

THE PRESENT

Your prana body lives in the present. Your mental and emotional bodies live in the past and future.

When you drop conditions for the present moment to be a certain way, then you are happy. Drop your expectations for the present. Get out of your own way.

Your circle of influence is your reaction to what is happening right now.

Let your heart be unconditionally open to whatever is present.

Come back to the present, again and again.

Conditionally present means that you are present only when God allows all of your circumstances to satisfy your desires.

THE FUTURE

How much of your life is dedicated to the future?

Don't focus on the result. Focus on your spirit.

You can waste your life energy getting or trying to get external things in the future. You live now—in the present moment—and there is no guarantee that you will be happy when you get what you desire.

YOGA ASANA

A posture is a place where you can practice stillness.

With asana, first quiet the body, relax the body, and then…relax the mind.

Asana withdraws the prana from your head and moves it through your body.

When you access the spiritual dimension of asana you move from thinking to experiencing.

Adapt your asana practice to service pranayama, prepare your mind for meditation and your heart for prayer.

Internalize your experience and connect with your body directly.

Yoga is an inner journey where you remove conflicts with yourself—reactive perceptions that you believe are real, such as when people prevent you from getting what you want, when you want it and at your speed. These perceptions create internal conflict.

MIND

The human mind is unique in the animal kingdom and empowers us to be creative, thoughtful, compassionate, and loving. It can also be a warehouse of negative emotions such as jealousy, anger, and self-doubt. Yogis have spent centuries trying to grasp exactly how mind plays a central role in creating our personal reality.

One aspect of reality is how mind organizes time. In the West, time is divided into sections to create projects and goals. You envision the future based upon timeframes. You have trained your incredibly flexible mind to accomplish great things using time as a yardstick to measure success. Unfortunately, time-oriented goals create problems. The problem is not the goal itself, but rather getting attached to a specific outcome.

It is easy to waste energy trying to achieve an outcome in the future. There is no guarantee of happiness when you get what you so badly desire. And, if you don't get what you envision, you set yourself up for disappointment. You live only in the present moment, and it is easy to forget that the journey is as important as the outcome. Because the mind is often successful, we tend to defer to the judgements it makes. Do not believe everything you think.

When Your Crazy Mind Controls Your Energy

Mind loves to do something. When you don't have a goal or time-oriented project, you might use the mind to worry. You can even worry about not having goals, that the calendar is not full, or all the terrible things that could…but have not yet happened. You lose your prana, your energy, when your mind dwells on things that are outside your circle of influence.

As you age, you discover there are a wide variety of things that are outside your control. The mind requires even more energy to deal with the unknown, and the result is often fatigue. Even worse, your subconscious mind accentuates the process. In dreams, your subconscious mind carries the storyline of the waking mind, adding another layer of fear and anxiety.

Your biological prana, or energy, is connected to your breath. When prana is unconscious it manifests as a tightness in the physical body. Usually this tightness occurs in the solar plexus, the Manipura chakra, which corresponds to your nervous and immune systems. The plexus is the concentration of the nerves in this region of the body. This is your personal power, your self-confidence, how you judge yourself and others. It spins out of balance when you feel threatened; or when rules restrict you, stifling your natural exuberance.

A common solution to address this combination of mental and physiological stress is with the use of alcohol, sex, television, surfing the social media feed...anything that gets you out of your mind. These distractions effectively create temporary harmony. Unfortunately, as soon as they wear off, they need to be used again. It is the reason they become addictions.

You need and deserve internal harmony. It happens naturally by helping your body get more energy. Return to breathing; deep, slow breathing combined with an intention of well-being. Intention is important because as you breathe consciously the breath carries the guided meaning of relaxation and health throughout your body. When you connect with your body, it anchors the mind into the present moment, and you heal. Your mind takes an unfiltered break, and your body gets the energy it needs to perform effectively.

Use Consciousness to Dismantle Habitual Reactions

The next step is consciousness. Consciousness is a tool you can use to become aware of and shapeshift reality. Consciousness is the ultimate rebellion against adopted reality. What is adopted reality? Your habitual patterns, *samskaras*.

The reality you are empowered to create is a feeling of joy in the present moment. The key is choiceless awareness. When something happens that pushes your buttons—the grocery store is out of your favorite food, someone cuts in front of you on the highway—practice catching yourself the moment you have a reaction. Train yourself to let go of the physical and psychological tension that builds inside your body. Learn to eliminate the buttons that trigger your reactions, not the button pushers—there are too many of them.

Life offers a series of therapeutic irritations. They are therapeutic because you can learn to dismantle the habitual patterns that come from flight or fight reactions based upon your experiences and reactions. If you don't let them go, they will continue to haunt you. Dissolve these karmic reactions. Learn to relax. Be free. Eliminate the reaction of "for or against" and the future remains open.

Don't stop making plans. Enjoy making plans, and then let them go. Do not focus on the result. Focus on your spirit and what it is telling you. Accept the unknown. Be comfortable with change and contradictory outcomes.

Responsibility, Intention and Outcomes

One teaching from many traditions relates to personal responsibility for the vision and creation of your life as it unfolds; and collectively the life, the dream, we share for planet Earth. This responsibility does not mean that you are at fault when things don't go right in your life. Unpleasant, unexpected, terrible events happen to everyone. The list is unlimited: a bad boss, loss of a loved one, a breakup, a health issue, a car accident.

These events, and the people involved, are not in your control. What is in your control is your reaction. Try not to carry the energy of an event, especially a spontaneous one, into your mind and body. Let it go. If something unpleasant occurs for a longer duration, you need to make a plan, move in a new direction. This is your responsibility.

When a rattlesnake bites you, go to the Emergency Room. The next day you can go to a shaman or psychologist to discuss why the snake attacked. It is the same with bad events. First deal with them; then reflect and try to understand if there is a teaching or lesson. What circumstances, emotions, actions, energy were connected to this event for you? Have you had similar experiences before? If you don't reflect on what has happened, there is a good chance it will happen again.

One way to change your life is with intentions. In Sanskrit the word for intention is *sankalpa*. It has a slightly different meaning than the English word. You get a new job. You marry your sweetheart. Clearly you intend to be successful with work, and have a long, happy marriage. These are time-oriented outcomes. Time-oriented because you imagine that over a period of time you will create a certain outcome with work and marriage. If you don't receive this outcome it is a disappointment; and you may blame yourself or another person.

Consider an intention to be timeless. It guides your actions. It is a direction rather than an outcome. Consider:

"I accept all the abundance the universe showers upon me." "My heart is always renewed and filled with joy." "I accept myself as I am and the world as it is." These will be true at any point during your life journey.

Begin a practice of Yoga Nidra relaxation to connect your intentions with your subconscious mind, creating harmony between what you think, say and do. Let your flexible mind find a new way to support you, and let consciousness create a pathway for a beautiful future. If you would like to experience a 28-minute session titled *Yoga Nidra for Health and Healing* visit **williameager.hearnow.com**.

One way to *be here now* is to feel the energy of an experience as it occurs. Allow the felt sense of all vibrations—singing, music, movement—to set into your awareness. Then, sink into the experience.

EXERCISE

Sound Vibration Quiets the Mind

Chant the mantra "OM" out loud—five times, slowly. Allow it to become a gentle and rhythmic *AUUUUM*. Let the sound move up from your lower abdomen. Allow the vibrations to resonate through your body...stomach, chest, throat and head. By focusing on the energy of sound, mantra, your mind and thoughts can settle into the background. You may notice that the energy of this sound actually moves through your body from the base of your spine up through your chest and towards the top of your skull. That's what OM is supposed to do. Move energy up through your central nervous system in a combination of cleansing and receptivity.

Chant for a minute. When you are done, sit quietly and see how the energy settles into your entire body. Be quiet and still. Experience the vibrations of the sound you have made. Experience the impact of the energy. Watch your breath. Don't control it. Observe. As the breath moves into your body simply acknowledge that consciousness is riding on top of the breath. Like a surfer on a wave. Don't worry about what the consciousness is supposed to mean. Don't give it definition. It comes in with the breath. Imagine that the breath is not only moving in and out of your lungs. It is moving, as it does, into all parts of your body. Your body is filling with this consciousness and the energy that it rides on. Shiva and shakti are moving into you.

Your breath is helping you relax. This is a space where you disappear. You are in unity with what is. In this experience you disappear to feel and experience the combined energy and consciousness of mantra. Mantras have specific energetic purposes, and you will feel it.

ATTENTION

When you put awareness on your sensations you enhance the energy flow in your body.

Attention has been conditioned to be dispersed and externalized...move it inward.

BELIEF

Everything you believe is a projection of your internal map.

Any belief you hold is a limiting belief.

When you are not in reaction you allow your prana to flow and do natural healing. You access energy that is trapped in your body, trapped by your thoughts and belief systems.

If you believe something very strongly, know that the opposite is also true.

≋

CHANGE

If you want to know what is at a destination, ask someone who has been there and is coming back.

≋

CHOICE

Choiceless awareness is choosing neither for nor against something based upon your past experiences. Before you can consciously choose what you want, or where you want to go, you must be choiceless to use consciousness.

≋

CONFLICT

Maintain harmony during conflict. Relax into the sensations of prana.

The external pressures of the world put pressure on you, and when you use your mind to solve the problems your prana suffers.

Whatever happens, you get the opposite as well. Happiness comes with sadness; but neither belong to you. You are not happiness or sadness.

≈

COMMUNICATION

Your presence as a listener changes the energy of the entire space.

When a listener lets go of their reaction(s) the energy field is clear for dialog. The listener becomes a mirror for what the speaker is saying.

Deep listening requires you to focus attention on the speaker, not on your upcoming response.

As a listener you wait to hear the other person. To see if their words match what you have in your mind. This allows you to judge them, agree or disagree with them. This is an intellectual and mental analysis; not an energetic, feeling-based reaction. When a person speaks from their heart you can hear them. This is right-brain listening where you connect with profound, simple truths you are already aware of.

≈

EGO

The ego judges the present based on what it experienced before.

Energy has intelligence, but it can't flow freely and do what needs to be done if ego is involved.

The egoic mind lives in separation from love which has no boundaries.

The ego jumps in to protect you from being hurt again. Frequently it does this in a way that enhances what hurt you in the first place. A misguided belief system about yourself. The result is that you keep this story and energy with you.

Spirit energy is your soul. If you use spirit energy to accomplish activities of the ego you can destroy your own soul.

You allow your ego to create a story about yourself with labels that make you an object. Then, you relive this story endlessly; and your friends sign up to collaborate.

Identify and then destroy your myths about yourself.

When you get yourself to a new space, hold it. The world will help you because they see it.

≈

EMOTION

Crying is not emotion. It is your time-based body on the way out.

Emotions are forms of energy that get stuck in your chakras.

Don't feed your spiritual hunger with emotional food.

Feelings and thoughts are the activities of the mind that come from samskaras.

≈

ENVIRONMENT

The environment you put yourself into, in your mind, creates your entire world.

～

GOALS

Don't make things happen, let things happen.

You must begin with what you want in the end. If you want peace in the future, you must start with peace and carry it with you. If you want love, be loving.

You think you can be happy by managing external affairs. You cannot manage what is outside of yourself. You need to manage your internal affairs.

Your "to do" list reflects insecurities about the future. You can never complete it because a new list arises the moment you finish one.

HABITS

Don't let your habits justify your disfunction. Empower yourself to be whoever you want.

When habits get built into your neuroglandular system, mechanical emotions are triggered.

People work their entire life to acquire enough security that their habits can be comfortable.

HARMONY

The absence of struggle is true fulfillment.

Use your breath to get out of your mind. Breathing brings you back to your physical body where you can fully experience the present moment. Your energy body is found by taking your awareness to your third eye, the ajna chakra, the point between your eyebrows in the center of your head, and feeling the physical sensations in your body.

JUDGMENT

Accept what is for what it is, not what you think it should be.

A good experience misunderstood is a bad experience.

The moment you doubt yourself you give power to doubt which completely overshadows the incredible capabilities you have.

When you judge yourself you injure your own heart.

Consider making no judgments, comparisons, or bargains and delete the need to understand.

Nature never judges. That is why you feel peaceful and at ease in nature.

~~

MIND

Every action you create stems from a thought, idea or concept in your mind.

The monologue in your mind has little to do with what is happening right now.

The energy that the mind produces affects the body. Over a lifetime it can create big problems or wonderful outcomes.

Allow your experience to transcend your knowledge.

You don't have to stop your mind. When you don't identify with it, it merges automatically.

Normally your mind dominates your prana.

Attune to the discovery of who you really are. Rest in awareness.

The mind categorizes everything, and it changes its view of the world to suit its needs.

The mind reacts to the present by comparing it to its own concept of the ideal future or ideal past.

You deal with the source of everything that happens—your mind.

Be a lion, not a dog. Throw a stick for a dog and they immediately chase it; throw a stick for a lion and the lion turns and looks toward you, the source of the stick in motion.

You choose to have external objects fulfill your desire for happiness. This is only a temporary solution. This misconception of what it takes to achieve happiness is a deception, a pollution of the mind; and this directly creates a pollution of the planet because we produce and purchase more objects than we need.

~

MIRRORS

Whenever you are with another person, what you see in them is a direct reflection of what you see in yourself at that moment.

Instead of changing the reflections of what you see in others, change yourself.

~

PATIENCE

Fulfillment simply means becoming whole.

False patience is when you think that by waiting you will get something that makes you happy.

When the stop light turns red it is not intentionally delaying you. It is only your impatience that creates stress in your mind and body. If an inanimate object can stress you out, imagine what a person can do. It really appears that they are doing something to you; but it is only your reaction that causes a problem. It is not what they are doing.

PERCEPTION

Your perception is a mirror of an internal map that you always carry with you.

Magical thinking is supported by practical understanding.

Notice what you say and don't contract to things you don't want to happen.

REACTION

Do not identify yourself with your reactions. Simply become a witness.

When the urge to react comes, let it go. Move to your breath.

Your first reaction is a reaction to an unresolved karmic past and your second reaction is a reaction to the reaction.

When you have a reaction, it is not a reaction to the event or the person, but to the original cause of that—a past fear or attraction. Release immediately.

RE-action is simply old habit patterns coming back. That is why re-action happens again.

Whenever you perform actions without attachment to the result, you are doing karmic yoga.

When someone is having a reaction then you must accept it; otherwise you are having a reaction to their reaction. Acceptance is the key—accept them, accept yourself.

Replace the reactive presence of your internal voice with the non-reactive presence of your spirit.

Eliminate the buttons, not the button pushers.

SELF-IMAGE

Step into the presence, but not the self-image you identify with.

Liberation is freedom from identification with your self-image. Your body, mind and ego.

Your image of yourself exists nowhere but in yourself. Where does it come from? The graveyard of your unresolved past.

SILENCE

It is in silence that you hear.

STRESS

When you are stressed your mind becomes a problem producing factory.

When you reject yourself, or your current situation you create stress.

Notice how stress creates distress.

Unresolved tension creates psychosomatic stress that gets built into your body and mind.

SUCCESS

The ego can push boundaries to achieve higher levels of success. The result is a stronger ego.

You are neither a success nor a failure. You are a divine being of light and love.

THOUGHTS

All thoughts to achieve or do something create conflict. Understand that you do not need to arrive to be successful.

What you create with your thought forms is what you see in the world.

Thoughts are not the problem. They come and go. Attachment to them creates a space-time event where you become a doer, and then the ego wants to create a result that is dependent upon space and time.

When the infinite manifests into form it has a beginning and an ending. Thoughts are also forms that have a beginning and an ending…simply watch them.

You don't live in the world…the world lives in you.

Thoughts are like clay, very malleable. Look how easy it is to create a thought that states, "I am not good enough," or "People don't like me." Be still and aware of your thoughts and energy.

Your mental thoughts can be an object of your awareness, the same as a pot of flowers. Look at them, observe them, and take notice of what they do—their shape and effect. Put them on the floor in front of you and watch the words as they fly around.

TOO MUCH TO DO

No one is keeping bliss away from you...you simply don't have time for it.

You do not solve a problem with the same mind that created the problem.

WORRY

You are already useful where you are...nothing is by accident here.

When you worry you are making a prayer that something bad should happen.

Expectations are reactions waiting to happen.

Don't contract to events or outcomes that bother you because it gives them energy.

YOGA NIDRA

Yoga Nidra takes your intentions, your sankalpas, into your chakras.

Your intentions are seeds that grow the trees of your entire life.

In Yoga Nidra, you release the stress that exists between you and yourself.

Yoga Nidra is a choiceless state where you neither go "for" or "against" anything.

In an alpha brain wave state, you remember better because you listen energetically.

HEART

The shape of a heart has represented the symbol of love for centuries. It was popular during the Renaissance when it was used in religious art depicting the Sacred Heart of Christ. The relationship between the physical heart, an organ that pumps 2,500 gallons of blood daily, and the feeling and energy of love is direct and immediate. The heart is where the energy of love emanates. This is the Anahata chakra which governs your actions as you reach out to touch and embrace others. When you hug someone, your arms reach out and form an energetic line directly connecting your heart to theirs.

When it is in balance, the energy of the heart allows emotions to flow like water. It encompasses acceptance, forgiveness, compassion. Unconditional love is unconditional. Pets offer an example of unconditional love. No matter what we do they love us. In relationships love can move from a state of unconditional to conditional. Because of fear or insecurity, you may become obsessive, jealous and envious. You may expect something in return for love as if it is a commodity to be exchanged. "I love you" morphs into "I love you as long as you love me."

The energy of love is instantaneous. A smile, a hug, a laugh, a helping hand—simple, spontaneous acts encompass all that love offers. You are empowered to share and receive the energy of love at any time. You can use your love to deeply care for other people; but you cannot live their lives for them, or your life through them. Everyone is responsible for themselves, and you have a unique direction and purpose in life.

The energy of love can rapidly move you from *thinking and doing* to a place of *feeling and being*. It takes practice to live in the heart center. To have a heart-felt reaction to events that occur in real time. You have spent so many years polishing your mind to analyze events and calculate responses that you usually go there first. In other words, you often block the heart.

You do not allow it to operate at full capacity.

Gratitude, Life and Ceremony

Expand your practice and move into feeling life. In my workshop on shamanism there are three aspects that create connection to heart.

1. Gratitude.
2. Everything is alive.
3. Ceremony.

Gratitude. The very moment you wake in the morning make a note of what you are grateful for, do not over think. Simply say to yourself one or two things that you are profoundly grateful for today and let this carry you forward. If you like, take your first three steps in the morning and make each step one of positive appreciation. Say out loud: "I am happy. I am healthy. I am generous."

Second, recognize that everything is alive. Everything. Your pets, of course. The fresh food you eat. Alive. You literally accept life energy when you eat food. Expand this feeling to the plants in and around your home. Go further and accept that while their energy is slow, that physical objects including your couch, the fence around your home, your car, the pavement, all have a molecular vibration that gives them life. Everything has an energy and an aspect of living. Extend your gratitude to every person, animal, plant, and mineral (the four worlds) you encounter. They all help you move forward on your journey.

Third, create ceremony. Ceremony is a process by which you open yourself. You connect with life and energy. There are thousands of ceremonies for many purposes in all traditions. Ceremonies to connect with ancestors; honor nature; access your higher self. You can create your own ceremony. The act of taking a shower in the morning can move from being a chore to becoming a ceremony of cleansing. Move a little slower and let yourself use the process of showering—undressing, letting sacred water run across your body, cleaning and drying—as a vehicle to honor your body.

The key for ceremony is to give intention to the process. For example, when you are about to eat say, "I thank (the Lord, Great Spirit, God) for this food and I thank this food for the energy it gives to my body." Ceremony only becomes an unpowerful ritual when it turns into a series of motions that no longer contain the spirit of the ceremony. You can access gratitude, connect with spirit and engage in ceremony in a few minutes. All you need to do is make the connection between what you are doing and the heart-felt energy of the process. Here is a ceremony that can help you move to your heart center.

EXERCISE

Open Your Heart and Balance the Inner and Outer World

A simple technique to balance your inner and outer world and open your heart. If you have a bolster or a blanket roll it up and place it in a position where you can lie down on it with the bottom near the base of your spine and the top either at the top of your spine or under your head (whichever is most comfortable). If the blanket or bolster is short, you may need to add a pillow under your head to keep it from tilting back. The blanket or bolster helps open your chest, your heart.

1. Lie down on the bolster or blanket (on the floor, yoga mat, couch, bed). Make sure your head is propped up so there is no strain on your neck.
2. Cross your arms over your chest...almost as if you are giving yourself a hug, but loosely.

3. Take a deep breath in and let it go with a big sigh.
4. As you continue to breathe deeply say silently to yourself, *"I am being surrounded by wings of love."* Continue for one or two minutes.

ACCEPTANCE

Your external world reflects your internal world. Watch what is happening.

There is no difference between your acceptance of yourself and your acceptance of others.

You cannot hold someone else responsible for your expectations. Dismantle your reactions so the other person can recognize their reactions.

You can say to yourself, "Whatever _____ (this person) does I fully accept it."

ANGER

The only reason you get angry is because you expect something; and you don't get it.

Anger is a secondary emotion. Notice that before you get angry, you experience a disappointment which derives from an unfulfilled experience. Instead of yelling, admit your disappointment to others and yourself. Eliminate the energy of anger with honesty.

ATTACHMENT

The more attachments you have in your life, the less you can dream.

CEREMONY

A ceremony is something you do that gives you joy for yourself. You can share this like seeds that grow with others.

Wake each day with gratitude; know that everything is alive and use ceremony to awaken and connect with spirit.

A ritual is a ceremony that has lost spirit.

COMMUNITY

When you fill yourself with love and gratitude you inspire others.

Give to others what you are seeking from them. Give acceptance, love, excitement, and passion.

CREATION

Dream. Don't start with your plan. Start with nothing because it opens all possibilities.

Planning itself is not the problem. Simply learn to be relaxed doing it.

You cannot see other opportunities when you use your energy to focus on a single, future-oriented goal. You lose access to the infinite creativity offered by your soul.

You are God in disguise.

DREAMS

The dreamer only has to dream it…not necessarily manifest it.

If you see a friend or relative in a dream, contact them.

If you are in a dream and you find yourself running away, stop, turn around and run towards any enemy to dissipate the energy.

FORGIVENESS

Forgiving is half of the solution…forgetting is the other half.

When you don't forgive you destroy your own life, not that of the other person.

Nobody ever hurt you the way you think they did... it is your interpretation based upon past events and patterns that create the hurt.

Forgiveness is not ego-based. "I hold you accountable, and now I let you go." Forgiveness arrives when you let go of all thoughts related to the story.

HEART

When you speak from your heart there is an energetic transmission that occurs. People feel it.

Make every moment of your life a complete celebration of your existence.

The greatest distance is never physical, it is between mind and heart. Speak from your heart, not your mind.

INTUITION

Listen to your knowing and step into the magic.

LIMITATIONS

Sometimes when you "hit your edge," the edge reinforces your limitations. Use the light of your consciousness to move forward...the witness has no edge.

LOVE

When you tap into love it becomes an inspiration for living.

Your body is a temple and your heart the altar.

You don't own love…you can only direct it.

Don't ask for love…simply be loving.

Through love everything is possible that is not possible through the medium of the mind.

When you are neither attracted or repelled by another person you can give them full love and compassion because you are completely open.

Who looks for love from others? Everyone who has separated from source and feels that approval from another will make them whole.

When you spend time and energy looking for love outside of yourself you need to control and manipulate the situation. This creates attachment. Your attention becomes narrow as you focus on the object of your desire. It is so delicious that you want more of it. You may even think that love comes from the other person. That is not it. It is energetic oneness, the connection of male and female energy in polarity.

MANTRA

Allow the energetic impact of mantra and prayer to move through you.

You can ride the sound of mantra to akasha—the infinite space that encompasses everything.

OUTCOMES

Focus your inquiry on the observer and not on the manifestations.

SURRENDER

Surrender is the outcome of devotion. When you surrender, devotion is included.

Surrender sounds like giving up, bowing to another force. It is true that you are giving up artificial control and bowing down to what the universe can offer directly to you.

YOUR STORY

Create opportunities to share your stories before you die.

Don't cheat yourself of your magnificence over bullshit.

SPIRIT

The sacred aspect of being human is your divinity. Your ability to connect with spirit to embody the loving essence of who you truly are. You are a spiritual being, a divine soul living in the third dimension. Spirit is your direct connection between body, mind, heart, and soul to a higher source. The source of all that exists. Because your spirit moves much faster than physical matter or events on this plane of existence, you can use spirit to change all aspects of your life.

The basis of change or movement requires that you be energetically clean. Then you can see clearly and create the world you want to live in from a neutral point of view where all possibilities exist. When you have, for example, a physical problem, or even a problem with your perception of yourself (depression, lack of confidence, or self-respect) it becomes an energetic pattern in your system long before you need a doctor.

The pattern is reinforced as a habitual pattern that you adapt and slide into. You can make dramatic shifts by changing the energy pattern that exists in your aura. The energy pattern is a blueprint or imprint (which can be a karmic imprint). You clean, envision a new pattern, and ask spirit to help bring in this new imprint. You do this again and again—until the vision you have becomes the new reality.

Clean and Protect Your Energy

Why do you need to clean? And what is it that you are cleaning? There is energy around you all day. Everything is in a state of receiving and radiating energy. It affects you, surrounds you, enters you, and changes your energy. Some of this energy is chaotic. For example, in most cities there is the energy of sirens, dogs barking, the energy of other people who may be in a hurry, upset, sad, angry, or worried about something in their life. Their energy touches you; and it is easy for some of it to move into your aura and chakras.

This is not who you are. Your natural vibration of harmony and love is temporarily upset.

Chaotic energy creates blockages in your body that prevent the free flow of energy. You must do two things:

- First, you must clean, just as you take a shower in the morning to clean the physical dirt, you must clean the energetic dirt and the blockages. One way to clean the energy of your body is with smudge. Another option is to use energy itself, as in the next exercise.
- Second, you must protect yourself. Just like you put on clothes, sunglasses, shoes and earplugs for your physical protection, you must protect your energy body. The following technique of *Putting Out The Roses* is one way to accomplish energetic protection.

EXERCISE

Golden Light For Energy Cleaning

Sit quietly in a comfortable, upright position with your feet on the floor. Connect with your breath. Begin to slow it down, breathing in and out of your nose. Close your eyes. Be aware of your crown chakra, the very center of the top of your head, and above this area. Visualize golden light, the color of morning sunlight. This magnificent color has been imprinted on you since the day you were born. Imagine a stream of golden sunlight moving down into your body through your crown chakra. It flows into your head, back through the center of your head to the back of your head and then down your spine.

As you breathe in, visualize the air bringing in life, vitality, energy, and love. Let your intention for health ride in on the in-breath. When the golden light reaches the base of your spine release the energy and begin your exhalation. Let your breath and the golden light flow up the front of your body, out your arms, and back up through your throat and out the top of your head. Release the energy. On your out-breath, exhale negativity, emotions that no longer serve you. If you do this slowly, consciously, you may feel the energy moving in your body. This exercise can be done for just a few minutes, or it can be used to guide you into a deeper state of relaxation and meditation.

EXERCISE

Putting Out The Roses for Energy Grounding and Protection

The Rose is one of nature's greatest gifts. There are fossils of roses that are 35 million years old. The Greeks and Romans identified the rose with the goddess of love, Aphrodite and Venus. As the queen of flowers, Mother Mary has been connected to the rose. The rosary borrows its name from the rose.

Energetically a rose is completely neutral. What that means is that it will take into itself any energy in a room that is out of balance. Take a rose and wave it closely around your head several times. Watch and see how the rose opens as it takes in the energy of your body or the room it is in. Here is a ceremony known as *Putting Out The Roses* which provides a layer of protection against external energies. It can come in handy if you are going into an environment that is filled with other people's energies, or if you simply need to ground yourself.

1. Close your eyes.
2. In your mind's eye, imagine a red rose.
3. Let it float out in front of your body by a foot and visualize its stem moving down into the earth.
4. Create a second rose in your mind's eye. Let this one move out to the right side of your body. Allow its stem to move down into the earth.
5. Now, a third rose. Move it behind your body and let it root its stem.
6. Finally, a fourth rose. Let it float out to your left; and let the stem set down into the ground.

Spirit Creates Reality

From an energetically neutral space you can move and use your personal free will to create and accept any reality. This is why under exactly the same circumstances one person can be utterly thrilled and happy, and another person completely miserable—because both realities are possibilities! Which one will you accept?

Because spirit moves faster than the speed of light it can do anything—instantly. It can go to the moon. It can sense the feelings of other people who are physically distant. It can envision a perfectly healthy body; and it can witness complete abundance.

The physical world you live in takes a little longer to change because the energy of objects is slower, heavier. It may take a little time in the physical plane. It starts energetically. You must be careful of your thoughts. Do not think, for example, "I am not happy."

When you think something negative, catch yourself. This is the first step in changing the energy. Stop and realize what you just did. Then think instead, "I am grateful. I am lucky. Look at the abundance and grace that the universe gives me today. How can I help other people?"

Share this space with other people. Greet people with a hug and let them feel your heart energy. Look them in the eyes and tell them, "I love you. I believe in you. You can do anything!" This opens their crown chakra, the Sahasrara. Energy flows and they feel great and grateful for your acknowledgement of their potential.

EXERCISE

Get Answers from Your Higher Soul

Because your soul is not bound by time or space, it can access and answer questions about the present, future or past. This ceremony uses images and energy to let you rapidly communicate directly with your higher soul and spirit for answers you may be seeking.

It is useful to understand the language of the soul and spirit. We live in a physical world. At this basic level of interaction there exists the molecular level of being. The language here is the physical, which has become the domain of scientists and physicians. As we move up one level, we enter the realm of the mind. Words are the language of the mind; and this modality resides with writers, poets, and psychologists. Next, we move to the level of the soul. The soul uses and responds to the language of images. It is one reason night dreams share powerful stories for your life.

Artists, educators, and meditators use images to share imagination (images in action) and carry inspiration and peace to the soul. Finally, at the level of spirit, the language of interaction is energy itself. Shamans and energy healers work at this level.

Level of Interaction	The Language	Primary Healers
Spirit	Energy is the language	Shamans, energy healers
Soul	Images are the language	Meditation arts
Mind	Words are the language	Psychologists
Molecular	The physical body	Physicians

Sit down and take your feet out of your shoes. Place your feet on the ground and your hands on your lap, pointing upwards to the universe. Close your eyes and do the following breathing exercise. Keep your eyes closed. On the count of two breath in deeply for three full seconds; one, two, three. Hold your breath in for a count of eight. Two, three, four, five, six, seven, eight. Now exhale profoundly. Do this exercise again. And one more time (a total of three times).

Now, with your eyes still closed go directly to your third eye, the ajna chakra. This is the middle of your head, the intersection point between your eyebrows, the tips of your ears, and where your tongue touches your palate. Visualize a beautiful space. A private room, a place where you can be totally alone, totally relaxed. It can be whatever you want. Beautiful furniture, a view of the ocean, anything. Now ask everyone else in this space or room to leave. Make sure you are totally alone in this space.

Now, imagine a golden, gilded globe above your head. Your soul. Ask your soul to come down into your crown chakra, into your ajna, down into your throat and into your heart chakra. Let it be in all these chakras but stop at the heart.

Now, ask your question. The more specific your question the more specific the response. "Will my meeting tomorrow at 3:15 with Jane be fruitful for both of us?"

Wait for the response.

There may be an image, or images, even an audio response.

Ask a second, follow up question. Wait for the response.

Now open your eyes.

Let your soul move back up and out through your crown.

What did you see or hear? You may need to interpret the visuals…if there is an animal, what is it doing?

ACTIVITY

No one has ever become enlightened by completing their to-do list.

CHANGE

Everything external is in perpetual change.

Let us all live in a collaborative creation of our shared future.

Stories motivate conversations which create opportunities.

Prana is the medium for change. It is not only pranayama, which focuses on the use of oxygen; it is breathing with consciousness that creates transformation.

Sometimes you want to stay in a process because you do not want to make a decision.

The caterpillar is happy with its horizontal, two-dimensional movement from left to right. It cannot comprehend the third dimension of vertical, free flowing flight. It does not know it will have or can use wings.

CONSCIOUSNESS

The purpose of yoga is consciousness. You use consciousness to relax and become still when you encounter a physical or mental blockage.

You can make any form a vehicle for consciousness— yoga, painting, cooking, dancing, singing. Practice what you love with love.

Consciousness is the ultimate rebellion against adopted reality. In the heart of consciousness arises the power of awareness that projects both subjects and objects. True essence lies deeper than outward form.

Connect the dots between prana, choiceless awareness, and movement.

Allow the felt sense of all vibrations—singing, music, mantras—to set into your awareness, then sink into the experience.

Collective consciousness can be group hypnosis.

If you live in victim consciousness you will attract people that make you a victim.

Your own feelings and thoughts are objects of your awareness. They can have a life of their own.

Consciousness is like the light of the sun which illuminates the moon. What is your consciousness shedding light on? You illuminate the world with your thought forms, and you are the seer of everything that comes into your field of awareness. Don't let your awareness become affected by what is happening around you. Just as space itself does not get affected by the movement of the planets and asteroids that move through it.

DANCE

Let prana move you and dance like the wind.

Know that life has both fixed and free dances. A baseball team has nine players arranged in a certain position. When the ball is hit, the dance flows spontaneously. Notice what movements are fixed and free in your life.

DESTINY

The whole universe takes you where you are supposed to be, and you begin to see it.

You have an authentic self with passion and talent, and it yearns for expression and recognition in this incarnation.

You can get what you want through listening to energetic guidance.

To evolve you need three things: first, a group to support you; second, ceremonies and spiritual practices and third, spiritual knowledge and a spiritual teacher.

If you receive an opening to follow a spiritual path you should do it. Divert and you can fall into distractions, habits, and addictions that place you in a new pattern that may take years, or lifetimes, to get back to the point you left off. Ask yourself, "How many times has God knocked on my door?"

ENLIGHTENMENT

When you realize that all you see is only light then you cannot like or dislike anything that changes in your perception because it is only more light. You become enlightened.

FREE WILL

Be strong in devotion and clarify your will. Make a Sankalpa and then finish it.

Animals live only with prana. Prana tells them what to do and they act. The downside is they have a lack of free will. The tiger cannot think, "Oh, I would like to be an elephant. He is so large!" Humans can think anything. It allows us to manifest infinite possibilities, and ties us into a world that is not always in harmony.

HEALING

Healing is a journey that you are on. It is not an intervention.

Detach the mind from the perception of the body so the body can relax and perform automatically in harmony.

You must be in the present to heal. The moment you think, "I am not at peace with myself" then you are on a treadmill.

Almost every health problem is an internal conflict that manifests as an external problem in the body.

Aspects of disease will not stick when the person they stick to no longer exists.

A blockage cannot fight you unless you fight back. Surrender and be present with what is.

The difference between healing and curing is that in healing you do not collude with a diagnosis.

Instead of treating a disease you bring energetic balance to yourself or a client.

There is one thing you need to understand and accept at the deepest level: perfect health is available to you right now.

Get your prana in balance and your health will naturally follow.

INTEGRATION

Integration happens here and now, not in the future.

Postures, chanting, and meditation all move you to an intention of integration.

As the sound of chanting OM disappears into silence, let your thoughts also disappear into silence.

You can ride the sound of mantra to akasha—the infinite space that encompasses everything.

Energy touches you through sound.

KARMA

If you clear a genetic imprint, a karmic imprint, you can avoid dealing with the issues on the physical level because you have cleared them energetically.

It is important to understand your karmic lessons so you can stop patterns.

Spirit manifests in the body to work out karmic patterns...to see, experience and overcome the obstacles you have put in your own way.

Your subconscious energy field is filled with your own reactive perceptions, your karmic body.

Your experiences are encoded into the perception of the distracted ego mind.

LIGHT

After a thousand years the darkest dungeon immediately transforms when light enters.

Light does not fight with darkness; it simply eliminates it.

MEDITATION

You spend a lot of your time trying to seduce or repel. Meditation brings you to a point of clarity.

Recognize that stillness is a form of expression of prana.

Meditation is a way of life, not something to be practiced as part of life.

Most people think that silence and stillness mean no action. Transfer your egoic mind into your prana body which is both active and passive simultaneously...create a dynamic stillness.

Know that your prana is your primary connection to God and stillness. This is the secret to connecting with God.

You may not be familiar with your internal landscape.

Children argue, intellectuals discuss, and a meditator worships in silence.

Simply allow conditions to be proper—like when you make your bed and simply lay down to go to sleep. It is the same with meditation, you just have to go to it.

NATURE

All worlds—human, animal, plant and mineral—contain consciousness and energy, but at different levels.

Ask a rock if it would like to be picked and discover what you feel.

Nature, divine mother, will take your roles away and soften your ego.

Spirit transforms into substance and substance evolves and returns to spirit.

PEACE

A large storm never bothers the sky. You are the sky, not the storms of your emotions.

When you are completely at peace with everything as it is, you are in harmony.

PRAYER

When you pray and release it completely…any holding onto a desire for or against the outcome…your prayer can enter the unified energy field where it can be heard by cosmic consciousness and acted upon. Step out of your mind and let "thy will be done."

SACRED SPACE

Every moment of your life is a sacred act, a sacred moment. Treat it as such and your life will unfold within sacred space.

Create sacred relaxation to open a doorway to sacred space where you connect to your divine nature.

Sacred space is anywhere you come into right relationship with the four directions and heaven and earth.

Use deliberate action to create, open and close sacred space so you can be conscious and awake.

SELF AWARENESS

You gain blessings when you allow yourself to be yourself.

The perceiver can change the perceived; and you can change other people by the manner in which you perceive them.

SLEEP

When we sleep at night we are all the same; then, when we wake, we separate ourselves.

SOURCE

Yogic techniques are forms that are designed to take you to the formless which you are.

Your connection with source depends upon who you identify with—yourself or a being that is a soul.

You are the creator of the universe that you live in.

When you connect with spirit you connect with love.

TIME

Time is the fourth dimension of space.

You forget you are a timeless being when you get stuck in time.

The past is only a human dimension, and it is personal.

Cause is invisible and effect is visible. These are the edges of time—the beginning and end of something. You create effects which become karmic teaching tools.

You go to a timeless dimension when you do not cause or determine the effect.

Reality is never a problem. The only problem is when you judge the present moment against the past, or your perception of an ideal future.

www.ThriveInside.net

Glossary of Terms

This book is intended to be a gateway to your evolution. Wherever you are there is still another step forward. As such, some of the techniques and terms may be new or unfamiliar. It is my hope that it will inspire you to dig further. Conduct research, go online, find a workshop. Here are a few definitions:

Ajna—the chakra energy center at the center of the head between the eyebrows.

Akasha—a Sanskrit word that means ether, the basis and essence of all things in the material world.

Anahata—the chakra energy center at the heart center.

Bhastrika—a breath technique often referred to as bellows breath or fire breath that involves rapid breathing.

Chakra—the energy centers of the physical body.

Ida—the energy channel that moves on the left side of the spine.

Kapalbhati—a breath technique that is referred to as the "skull cleaning breath" and uses both forced breathing and relaxation.

Manipura—the chakra energy center at the solar plexus.

Mantra—a word and/or sound repeated to aid concentration in meditation or to change energy.

Mudra—a gesture using the hands or body that creates a seal. They facilitate the flow of energy for specific purposes. When you connect your thumb to your first finger it is called the Gyana Mudra and can increase focus and concentration.

Nadi—a term for the channels through which the energies of the physical body move.

Pingala—the energy channel that moves on the right side of the spine.

Polarity—a state of harmony when male and female energies are in balance and you are connected to your higher self.

Prana—the energy that moves in all things.

Pranayama—breath control techniques.

Sahasrara—the crown chakra energy center at the top of the head.

Samskara—habitual patterns, impressions, ideas, or actions which make up our individual conditioning.

Sankalpa—an intention formed by the heart and mind and effectively achieved with yoga nidra.

Shakti—the cosmic energy which represents dynamic forces that are thought to move through the entire universe in Hinduism.

Sushumna—the energy channel that moves from the base of the spine to the tip of the head at the center of the body.

Yoga Nidra—a yogic technique, known as the sleep of the yogi, that creates a state of deep relaxation where body, mind and spirit are connected and in harmony.

About the Author

My path with yoga began in 2001 as I discovered how poses and breath work have a dramatic effect on body, mind and spirit. As the spiritual aspects of yoga opened to me, I added yoga nidra and chakra work to the asana practice. The Amrit Yoga Institute and Yogi Amrit Desai have been a key source of my personal growth. I also studied with shamans around the world, and have had teachers from many traditions including Lakota, Dine', Mayan, South African and Siberian. I am passionate about teaching in a manner that is fun and meaningful for participants.

I have taught at numerous studios, Yoga Journal Conferences and my writings and articles have been featured in *Desh-Videsh, Natural Awakenings, Shape, Tathaatsu, Wisdom Magazine and Yogi Times.* I lead workshops on yoga, personal transformation, healing and yoga nidra for groups and individuals.

Books

Thrive Inside: Transformative Secrets of Spiritual Masters, Gurus and Shamans
Available on Amazon.com.

Workshops

The following workshops are four hours each. See ThriveInside.net for more information.

- ➤ Yoga Nidra: Realize Your Intentions, Manifest Your Dreams
- ➤ Yoga Nidra with Live Hammered Dulcimer
- ➤ The Chakras: Access Health and Healing
- ➤ Dance Like the Wind: Body, Mind, Heart and Spirit
- ➤ Introduction to Shamanism: Teachings of Lakota, Dine', Mayan and Siberian Traditions

Online Videos

The Chakras: An Experiential Workshop
vimeo.com/ondemand/thechakras

Secrets of Nature: The Basics of Shamanism
vimeo.com/ondemand/shaman

Contact

www.thriveinside.net/contact.html

Made in the USA
Columbia, SC
12 March 2021

34372346R00068